# JULIAN SEAMAN

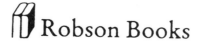

Robson Books

Also by Julian Seaman and published by Robson Books

*Horse Laughs: The Ups and Downs of Three-Day Eventing*
*Showing Off: The Lighter Side of Show-Jumping*

Designed by Harold King

First published in Great Britain by Robson Books Ltd.,
Bolsover House, 5-6 Clipstone Street, London W1P 7EB

Copyright © 1988 Julian Seaman

**British Library Cataloguing in
Publication Data**

Seaman, Julian
    Turfed Out
    1. Racehorses. Racing — Humour
    798.4'00207

ISBN 0-86051-526-5

Typeset by JCL Graphics, Bristol
Printed in Great Britain by
St. Edmundsbury Press Ltd.,
Bury St. Edmunds, Suffolk.

# CONTENTS

'I would destroy this book once you have read it.'
Henry Cecil

## Acknowledgements

I have enjoyed collecting material from many sources and people, I particularly want to thank Peter Willett, Nicky Henderson and Jane Ratcliffe for all their help, as well as Bernard Parkin for the cartoons and Susan Rea for trying to sort things out.

Cover photograph: © Kit Houghton
Back cover photograph of the author by Katie Colvin.
Steeplechase photograph © Sport and General.

## Bibliography

Among the books I consulted were: *Lester*, Claude Duvel (Granada Publishing); *Lambourn, Village of Racing*, Alan Lee (Arthur Barker); *Jump Jockeys*, Alan Lee (Ward Lock); *Pigsticking*, Willie Rushton (Queen Anne Press); *The Racey Bits*, Mark Siggers and Chris Williams (Jarrold); *Great Racing Disasters*, John Wellcome (Arthur Barker); *Short Heads and Tall Tales*, Lester Piggott and Roy David (Stanley Paul); *Tales of Racing and Chasing*, Terry Biddlecombe (Stanley Paul); *Jockeys of the 70s*, Tim Fitzgeorge-Parker (Pelham); *Born Lucky*, John Francome (Pelham); *Tales From the Weighing Room*, John Buckingham (Pelham); *Turf Account*, Steve Smith Eccles (Queen Anne Press); *150 Years of the Aintree Legend (Kingsclere Leisure); The World of Flat Racing*, Brough Scott and Gerry Cranham (World Books); *Hedges and Hurdles*, Roger Munting (Allens); and *The Sporting Repository*, an antique volume that gives some idea of the alarming way things used to be done.

# Foreword

## by Nicky Henderson

After taking an irreverent look at Three-Day Eventing and Show Jumping in his first two books, *Horse Laughs* and *Showing Off*, it was only going to be time before Julian Seaman gave our serious business of horse racing the same treatment.

*Turfed Out*, like the previous books, is full of anecdotes, cartoons, spoofs and photos. It covers all aspects of the Sport of Kings, but in the author's inimitable style.

Although Julian is really a retired three-day event rider, his thorough research went beyond the call of duty when he rode once round the Grand National course in the Foxhunters' Chase — (albeit at the fourth attempt in four years to conquer the first fence, and with a lot of help from the Grandstand.) The format of his books allows a chuckle from a casual random dip, either before turning out the light or pulling the chain.

# Motion is important

A sleeping person induces respect, almost as much as a dead one. So that even the Greek gods, when they eavesdropped on naked girls asleep, dared at the most, a kiss. Love in action presents itself as a combat; each motionlessness makes his excitement die down. Motion breeds the fiercest and quickest fulfilment. Two young persons, after a long gallop, may tie their sweating horses to a tree in the forest, tumble into the grass and at once possess each other, continuing the rhythm of the ride.

*Emil Ludwig — 'Of Life and Love'*

8

**hip·po·pot·a·mus** (hip´ə pot´ə məs) *n.,* *pl.* **-mus·es, -mi**
(-mi´), **-mus:** see PLURAL, II. D. 1 [L., < Gr. < *hippos,* a
horse + *potamos,* river] a large, plant-eating mammal
with a heavy, thick-skinned, almost hairless body and short
legs: it lives chiefly in or near rivers in Africa
**hip·py¹** (hip´ē) *n.,* *pl.* ... [Slang] same as ...

# THE WAY
# WE WERE

After the first race meeting at Leopardstown on 27th August 1888, a story ran in the national papers the next day, 'Sacred to the memory, Leopardstown, brutally and foully strangled at birth by gross incompetence, bungling and mismanagement.' The site had been bought for £20,000 by an Englishman, Captain George Quin, who had laid out a course to resemble Sandown. He failed, however, to provide adequate access, and the only entrance was a rickety bridge a yard wide. He also made the unforgiveable mistake of charging the press corps.

The Romans are recorded as having run horse races at Wetherby in 210 AD.

The first recorded trophy for a horse race was a wooden ball, presented at Chester in 1512.

The idea of racing three-year-olds began in the eighteenth century, and by 1790 two-year-old racing had developed.

In Tudor England, jumping was almost impossible because of the construction of saddles, which had very high pommels.

Because early racing started with heats, a chase at Waltham Abbey in February 1836 was reputed to have started at the walk, with a galloping ensuing only over the last of the four miles.

In the early days of steeplechasing, Hertfordshire was the national centre of the sport, but there was also a popular course for both flat and jump racing in London at Notting Hill, called the Hippodrome.

The first fence of the Prince of Wales Cup in an Edwardian Army point to point steeplechase at Arborfield Cross, near Reading.

# SOD'S LAW

One British jockey, having ridden a winner in Australia, was in the process of riding a second in his hotel room that evening when the phone rang, and he found himself being interviewed live on local radio!

In the early days of racing, horses were 'bled' by vets after a race — often with tragic consequences.

Until legislation in 1985, betting shops were required by law to be unattractive places to discourage people from spending too long in there.

In 15 seasons, John Francome lost 460 days through injury.

Although in theory jockeys are not allowed to bet, in the 1921 National the winner finished alone, when all the others had fallen or pulled up. But an amateur — Harry Brown — who owned, trained and rode his horse, The Bore, and, in an anomaly was, as an amateur, allowed to bet, remounted to finish second and pick up his each-way wager.

In a race at Ascot, Ron Atkins had a fall in a novice chase. Unhurt, he hitched a lift back in the course car and was dropped off near the finish. The race was over, but Ron was knocked unconscious by a loose horse — the horse he had been riding in the race.

Impossible to please: Fulke Walwyn trained the first five winners on a six-race card for owner Dorothy Paget on 29 September 1948 — Legal Joy, Langis Son, Jack Tatters, Endless and Loyal King. The sixth, Loyal Monarch, was only just beaten in the final race. However, Miss Paget's reply to press enquiries was only 'I'm disappointed at getting beaten in the last.'

John Francome retired in 1985 after a freak accident on the horse The Reject, getting his foot caught in the stirrups.

In one week in 1986 Captain Tim Forster lost three of his better horses. Amazingly at the end of the same week, the trainer and his jockey Hywel Davies registered a four-timer, illustrating the ups and downs of racing.

**Mam or 'mammy'.**

# PEOPLE

King James I was very keen on racing, but it was Charles II who became the only monarch to win a race. He won the Newmarket Town Plate in 1671, amongst other races.

Top lady jump jockey Gaye Armitage was nearly christened Gigi (nay!). Her parents lost their nerve at the font, but she has been known as Gee ever since. Her greatest racing moment to date came when she won at the Cheltenham Festival on a horse called Gee-A.

Captain Becher of Aintree fame, though a 'gentleman' rider, was one of the first paid jockeys. He in fact won an earlier race at Aintree before falling in the inaugural Grand Liverpool Chase (the Grand National) and collecting immortality.

An early race entrepreneur — Thomas Coleman — introduced hurdle racing to his meetings 'to please the ladies'.

An early sporting artist, Ben Marshall, moved to Newmarket for better prospects. He wrote, 'I have good reason for going. I discover many a man who will pay me fifty guineas for painting his horse, who thinks ten guineas too much for painting his wife'.

To raise money to save the Grand National, racing personalities Brough Scott, Lord Oaksey and Oliver Sherwood ran in the London Marathon in 1983. Oliver, just a few days after completing the National, himself 'broke down'!

Women were not officially permitted to train racehorses, though they often did so behind the name of their head lads, until in 1966 Florence Nagle began proceedings to sue the Jockey Club. She obtained her licence on 29 July that year.

# FIRSTS

Ascot racecourse was started by Queen Anne in 1711 — with the first ever 'Royal Ascot' on 11 August of that year.

The first recorded steeplechase was a match between Mr O'Callaghan and Mr Blake from Buttevant Church to the steeple of the church of St Leger, in Ireland in 1752. An early wager at that time between Sir Charles Turner and the Earl of March stipulated a course of ten miles and forty fences, with fences of 4ft 4in to be completed in one hour.

The first recorded race of more than two runners was in 1792 in Leicestershire.

The first recorded hurdle race was thought to have taken place in 1821, though George, Prince of Wales, Mrs Fitzherbert and ten Dragoon Guards reputedly raced for fun over sheep hurdles some time before.

The first steeplechase at Aintree was held in 1836 on the land which was then owned by Thomas Lynn, who also ran the Waterloo Cup for coursing. But it was 1839 when 50,000 spectators watched the first Grand Liverpool Chase.

In 1835 a steeplechase was first held at Cheltenham — a four-miler including a five-foot wall.

It was only in the latter part of the nineteenth century that enclosed park courses, with artificial fences and admission charges, were introduced. Sandown Park was the first of these; it maintained its reputation for innovation when it later became the first racecourse to have public loos.

Point-to-point racing was invented as an antidote to the by-then formalised sport of chasing. The first point-to-point was run over open country in 1870 by the Atherstone Hunt.

# ASCOT

## Circa 1894

H.M. The Queen is reputed to have told trainer Noel Murless that she didn't like ill-mannered little b★★★s riding for her, after Lester Piggott dashing off to change for the next race, had barely acknowledged her. This was after being placed on one of her horses at Ascot.

# BETTING FOR FUN AND PROFIT

but

Jockeys lash whip rules

and

GET

## GOOGLY FROM THE BOOKIES

£ £ £ £ £ £ £

One of the most popular winners at the Cheltenham World Jockey's Championship in 1984 was a tiny Japanese jockey called Shinobu Hoshinoi. Unknown here as he might be, he earns about £400,000 at home riding only about 60 horses in a season.

It was his riding of a horse, called ironically, Stopped which got John Francome pulled up in front of the stewards at Cheltenham. This opened up the speculation about his relationship with the bookie John Banks, which led to a six-week ban and a £750 fine for allegedly giving Banks confidential information.

With a first wage of two shillings and sixpence, Joe Mercer was fined sixpence for every time he fell off.

Piggott meanness: A lad was trying to get £10 out of Lester for leading in a winner. Lester replied he couldn't hear the lad as it was his deaf side. The lad spoke to the other ear and said, 'Lester, you said you'd bung us twenty quid,' to which Piggott replied, 'It was only a tenner a second ago.'

Oops! A steward was congratulating a trainer's wife after their horse had come in at very generous odds. The steward asked how much money they had on the horse, to which she disarmingly replied, 'Not a penny. (My husband) hasn't had a bet since he stopped riding.'

After a stewards' enquiry at Goodwood one year, the press asked a grim-faced Lester Piggott what the result had been. 'I'll tell you for £100,' he said. He'd just been fined £100.

The stud fee for the great Arkle's sire Archive was only 49 guineas.

£ £ £ £ £ £ £

# BOG
# 🍀🍀🍀🍀 STANDARDS 🍀🍀🍀🍀

Witnessed recently at the Cheltenham Festival, an Irishman withdraws £50,000 in cash and turns to his friend, 'Right, that's seven grand a race and we've a bit left to have a drink.'

In 1986, the *Financial Times* reported a sudden, damaging run on the Irish punt during the early part of March. This puzzled analysts, as the punt had been performing quite well against the pound. It transpired that the annual Irish pilgrimage to Cheltenham had actually unbalanced a nation's currency!

The Irish really do love horses: with a population of around three and a half million they have approximately 7,500 brood mares, or one to every 500 people; the ratio in mainland Britain is approximately one to every 7,250 people.

Some Irish punters brought their car over on the ferry from Dublin to Liverpool and set off down the M6 for Cheltenham. They ended up in Wales, thinking that the HR (Holiday Route) signs were directing them to the Horse Racing!

'If that fella's horses were half as good as he reckons, they'd be twice as good as they are.'

Irish sales talk for one of the author's point-to-pointers, 'He's a grand lepper, he is — I haven't seen him jump m'self.'

🍀🍀🍀🍀🍀🍀🍀🍀🍀🍀🍀🍀🍀🍀🍀🍀🍀🍀🍀🍀🍀🍀🍀🍀

# LAYTOWN RACES

'You know Sean—there's something very
attractive about racing at Laytown!'

NATIONAL THEATRE NT IN THE WEST END

By arrangement with GENIUS PRODUCTIONS

ROBERT BURNS & PETER BALDWIN
present

GEOFFREY HUTCHINGS · TOYAH WILLCOX

KEN STOTT · DESMOND BARRIT · CYRIL SHAPS
and

ALISON FISKE · NICHOLAS LE PREVOST

in

THE NATIONAL THEATRE PRODUCTION OF

# THREE MEN ON A HORSE

by

JOHN CECIL HOLM & GEORGE ABBOTT

with

BOB CARTLAND & MICHAEL BEINT

and

RUDDY L DAVIS · ERROL EDMONDSON
COLETTE HILLER · MARIANNE MORLEY
JOHN PRIESTLEY · ROBERT RALPH

MUSIC BY THE BOB BURNS QUINTET
DESIGNED BY SAUL RADOMSKY
LIGHTING BY ROBERT BRYAN
DIRECTED BY JONATHAN LYNN

## VAUDEVILLE THEATRE

Directors: MICHAEL CODRON, DAVID SUTTON
STRAND LONDON WC2. TEL: 01·836 9987/5645

# HORSES

All 200,000 thoroughbred racehorses today can trace their parentage back to three sires. Eastern horses were thought faster, so these were imported for stud:

1  **The Byerley Turk.** This horse was taken by Capt. Byerley at the Siege of Buda in 1688, and subsequently ridden by him at the Battle of the Boyne.

2  **The Godolphin Arabian.** This was foaled in the Yemen in 1724 and given to Louis XV. It was imported c. 1730 before ending up at Earl Godolphin's stud near Newmarket.

3  **The Darley Arabian.** This horse was bought by a Mr. Thomas Darley at Aleppo in c. 1703, and sent to stud in Yorkshire.

It was this mix of Arabian and English stock which produced the thoroughbred.

In 1840 a race was open to all except Lottery. He was barred because he was the best horse of his day, and the winner of the first 'National'.

Steeplechasing only achieved social respectability in 1900, when the Prince of Wales's horse, Ambush II, won the Grand National.

After his amazing Grand National feats, Red Rum has since earned more as a personality (Red Rum Limited) than he did racing.

Lord George Bentinck invented the horsedrawn horsebox to take his horse Ellis to the 1836 St Leger, to the horror of the bookies who had seen the horse in Sussex earlier that week.

Newmarket's 'Rowley Mile' is named after Charles II's favourite horse.

# THIS SPORTING LIFE

Jockey in unsaddling area at Huntingdon when horse has trailed in at the back of the field: 'That's not his trip, guv'nor, I think he'd get three miles.'
Incredulous trainer: 'Three miles. He wouldn't get three miles in a **** ing horsebox.'

Two disgruntled, evidently losing, punters had been consoling themselves in the bar at Kempton, and after the meeting were walking it off on the course. 'I don't know what these bloody jockeys get paid for,' said the first punter, scowling at the nearest fence. 'Any bugger could jump these things. I could do it myself without a horse.'
'Go on then,' said his friend, peering owlishly through the gloom. 'Jump that one.'
The first punter divested himself of his race glasses, took a run at the nearest fence and cleared it triumphantly with feet to spare — and landed in the water!

The highest and lowest in racing have something in common. A young groom at a point-to-point yard one day received a brown envelope in the post, and asked in all innocence, 'What is the Inland Revenue?'

Several soccer stars have owned racehorses, but one sensibly stipulated to his trainer that he would rather his didn't race on Saturdays, as he was likely to be busy.

At a race meeting in Lahore in 1988, the racecard also included rules of the Turf Club. Rule 6 stated that betting was illegal and that offenders would be punished. Nevertheless, there were 80 on-course bookies. When one of these bookies was asked whether successful bets were subject to tax as in Britain, he logically replied, 'How could they be? Betting is illegal.'

# Anything you can do...

# TRUE FACTS

Peter Willett, the international breeding expert and author, was asked to set the 'specialist subject' questions on 'The English Thoroughbred' for the TV quiz 'Mastermind'. The contestant claimed to have read all his books so, duly flattered, Willett produced questions which could all have been answered with a good knowledge of these books. Unfortunately, the lady contestant scored bottom marks.

One early series of races which began in 1843 in the Vale of Aylesbury was called the 'Aylesbury Aristocratic Steeplechases' — made famous by the prints of Henry Alken.

The Cheltenham Gold Cup was introduced in 1924, but in those days was a modest race. The Champion Hurdle started in 1927.

In 1842, a legal test case was brought in a gambling dispute based on the claim that a steeplechase was not a proper horse race. The judge ruled that it was.

During the Second World War, both the Derby and the St Leger were run over the July course at Newmarket.

The 1942 Cheltenham Gold Cup was run in dense fog, but radio commentator Raymond Glendenning had to pretend he could see what was happening so as not to give away the weather conditions to enemy radio 'hams' in Europe.

Lester Piggott's father trained the 1963 Grand National winner Ayala for Mr Teazy-Weazy Raymond, the hairdresser, at 66 – 1.

Lester Piggott first rode in a race at the age of 6.

Henry Alken's famous prints of moonlight steeplechase are probably based on his imagination — the races were said to be run 36 years before he depicted them.

# THIS SPORTING LIFE

In the early nineteenth century, steeplechasing was considered a slightly better spectator sport for the populace than bull-baiting, which was outlawed in 1840.

The term 'gentleman rider' was superseded by 'amateur rider' in the 1870s — though most of these amateurs readily accepted money for riding.

Despite its almost 270 racecourses and excellent prize money — as well as a lottery, the Tierce, which sells millions of tickets — French racing suffers from public indifference. In 1968 the only mention of the result on the TV news of the French Derby, run at Chantilly, was 'bon Tierce à Chantilly, le 17, le 4 et le 13.' There was no reference to the names of the horses or their riders.

One year a trainer driving to Aintree passed a funeral procession. Later that day, his horse won, so the next time he went to Aintree he drove around looking for a funeral and his horse won again.

In New Zealand, pre-race instructions are imparted in the weighing room to jockeys who then go by themselves to the paddock and are expected to vault on.

There is an animal protection league in the USA which maintains that stud farm breeding is 'organised rape' and recommends artificial insemination instead.

Arthur Thompson, who won the 1948 National on Sheila's Cottage and again with Teal in 1952, was riding at Southwell one day when another jockey, Arthur Freeman, came up on his inside. Thompson just reached over and pulled the bridle off Freeman's horse!

In one French jumping race a few years ago, 15 of 22 jockeys were found to have been bribed by the Mafia.

(V) Cursorial mammal of the Obscene Age. First recognisable specimen of The Noble Animal as such.

(VI) Early horse of the Must'ang Dynasty (China). Very valuable and docile (a child could break it).

(IV) Mesozoic Neohippos. Much better bred, with only three toes; mane nearly in right place but tail still definitely wrong.

# THE GRAND NATIONAL

In 900 AD the Vikings cleared a forest near Liverpool, leaving just one tree. Hence the name of the Grand National site: Aintree.

'They might have left us one each!'

The first National — the Grand Liverpool Steeplechase — was won in 1839 by Jem Mason on Lottery. A horse called Conrad fell into a stream, thus ensuring immortality for his rider — Captain Becher.

In 1865, a five-year-old flat racehorse, Alcibiades, won the Grand National, having never before jumped in public.

When Mrs Mirabel Topham sold Aintree racecourse she took as a memento the finishing post, which she erected in her garden in the Isle of Wight.

It's incredible to think that the cost of one flat race yearling at Keeneland could buy an entire Grand National field.

In 1879 four brothers — Tommy, Harry, Willie and Johnny Beasley — all rode in the Grand National. Tommy did best, riding Martha into third place.

The smallest Grand National winning horse, 15.2hh Battleship, was ridden by both the youngest and the tallest winning jockey: 17-year-old and 6ft 3in tall Bruce Hobbs.

Jay Trump, ridden by American amateur Tommy Smith, won the 1965 Grand National, but his first preparation race in England, which the horse also won, was Fred Winter's first winner as a trainer.

Although the Topham family managed Aintree racecourse for generations, Mirabel Topham, who at the height of her Aintree rule weighed 18 stone, started off as a Gaiety Girl — and acted under the name of Hope Hillier.

The Grand National became a handicap race in 1843: before then, all horses had to carry 12 stone.

In 1840 a wall of 4ft 8in was specially built on the Grand National course, in front of the grandstand, yards from where the Chair is today. In 1845 an artificial water jump was added, and still exists.

# BOG STANDARDS

An Irish trainer, James 'Paddy' Drislane, working in the north of England at the end of the nineteenth century, liked to keep his horses' schooling performances as secret as possible from the touts. He is reputed to have held a steeplechase trial by moonlight. History doesn't relate what he paid his schooling jockeys!

Having been told that a chance ride on an Irish horse was safe enough because the animal 'jumps houses', it promptly fell at the first. The jockey explained to the puzzled trainer afterwards, 'Sorry, sir, he tripped over the f***ing chimney pot'.

Irish auctioneers Goff's dropped a bombshell on the racing establishment in 1987 by announcing they were to sponsor a £1-million race in Ireland, making it Europe's richest race. It was the conditions which caused the outrage. The race would be exclusively for two-year-olds which had been purchased at the Goff's Yearling Sales. Because of these entry restrictions, 'the establishment' retaliated by not conferring Group I status on the race.

James Drislane had one disastrous Newcastle meeting. A horse which he entered, but specifically didn't want to win, trotted up, because the completely inexperienced lad, deliberately put up to give the horse a bad ride, couldn't hold it.

The trainer then backed a mare of his which liked firm ground. Before the race there was a downpour, so he laid off all his bets, but the horse unexpectedly won.

On the way to the station the following day, he intended to buy his wife a present. He went for his purse, and found that he had been pickpocketed. At this moment, an organ grinder's monkey landed on his shoulder. Drislane fell backwards through the plate glass of a jeweller's window.

He hurled the monkey back at the grinder, then set about the chap with a walking stick. A policeman appeared, and Drislane was charged with damage and assault.

An Irishman who pulled off a betting coup on a horse whose previous form on the card was registered 'FFFP' (ie, three falls in a row and then pulled up) claimed he thought its past form was brilliant: 'First, First, First & Pissed It'.

In an early challenge race in Ireland, the favourite, Black & All Black, owned by Sir Ralph Gore, a cavalry officer stationed at the Curragh, was well beaten by the local horse Irish Lass, whose cause was helped by wearing a rosary round her neck for the race.

An incorrigible Irish racing rogue of the 1840s, Thomas Ferguson, brought his star horse Harkaway to England, admitting happily about Ireland, 'there's nothing left here to cheat'.

# An Open Book!

**IT'S THE RULES THAT COUNT**

Only when you have read his rules and considered them in their entirety will you understand why you *must* bet with

## DUGGIE

# THIS UNSPORTING LIFE

One good old-fashioned punt which looked as if it might go wrong was partially saved by some outrageous quick thinking. Together with his cronies, a professional backer who had a horse running in a handicap at Loughborough some years ago put a stack on the horse. It was ten lengths in front at the last fence and all was going well. The party was standing by the judge's box, in those days a free-standing army type sentry box, to cheer their horse in.

It up-ended at the last and all seemed lost. The punters, however pushed over the sentry box with the judge inside and sat on it. With no judge, the stewards had to declare the race void, the bet was saved and the team eased back into the crowd.

One outrageous betting fraud was nearly accomplished just before the First World War. The perpetrators were never discovered, but their plot has become a legend.

On a bank holiday, when there is often a great deal of racing, a punter at the Hurst Park meeting was laying considerable sums on another meeting at somewhere called Trodmore Park. The bookie hadn't heard of Trodmore Park, but the punter waved a copy of *The Sportsman* and there indeed was the meeting. Trodmore Park never existed, but the fraudsters had a 'plant' in the paper's office, who, taking advantage of the extra bank holiday activity, slipped the page through.

The bookie's suspicions saved him, however, and the mystery punters never returned.

In a Hong Kong racing scandal in 1974, one poor horse was discovered to have been doped to go slower by one gang and faster by another.

# OLD CROCKS CORNER

Crockford, owner of the St James's gambling hall, owned the second favourite in the Running Rein Derby of 1844 — Ratan. The horse was both doped and 'pulled' in the race and on hearing this, Crockford had apoplexy and died two days later on Oaks day. Crockford and his cronies had a substantial joint bet on the Oaks, but his death would have invalidated the wager.

The cronies worked out a plan. One went to Epsom for the race, armed with a carrier pigeon to take the results of the race to the now very-deceased Crockford. The backed horse, Princess, won, so part two of the plan was put into action.

Crockford's body was brought down, dressed up and sat in the window of his club as 'proof' of his well-being. The winnings were collected, but sadly, with such a good story to tell, someone spilled the beans, and not for the first or last time, the reputation of the 'sport of kings' took a serious dent.

Bookmakers are men who make their living by betting, as distinct from punters, who lose theirs by the same process.

**Brown trouser sport.**

# THE GRAND NATIONAL

Sea Pigeon won a flat race (The Ebor Handicap, over a mile and three-quarters) and the Champion Hurdle in the same year, 1979 — with the same jockey, Jonjo O'Neill.

Although ungelded horses are unusual in chasing—for obvious reasons—Red Prince II ran in the Grand National early this century and the entire horse Battleship won in 1938 and the French-bred Fortina won the Gold Cup in 1947. Happily, little damage seems to have been done, as they both went on to become successful sires.

After winning the 1967 Grand National on the outsider Foinavon, John Buckingham was asked to appear the following day on stage at 'Sunday Night at the London Palladium', compèred by Bob Monkhouse. Horse, jockey and horse's pet goat also paraded in front of Buckingham Palace and up The Mall.

Before his first Grand National in 1951, Fred Winter was bet by the senior jockeys that he wouldn't get past Becher's first time round. He fell two fences further on and returned to the weighing room to collect his winnings.

The 1919 Grand National was actually run at Gatwick, where the airport now is, and was called the War National Chase.

When Terry Biddlecombe first rode in the Grand National in 1960 on Aliform, he turned to fellow jockey Taffy Jenkins and asked which fence was Becher's. He had already jumped it, however, without realising.

# PEOPLE

St George was reputed to have slain the dragon up on the Berkshire Downs near Lambourn.

The stables at Tully (the Irish National Stud) were laid out at the turn of the century by an eccentric Englishman, Lord Wavertree, who ordered the boxes positioned so that the horses could study the stars!

The dog-leg course of the Cesarewitch starts in Cambridgeshire and ends in Suffolk, two and a quarter miles away.

The official birthday for all horses is New Year's Day.

Irish breeder to purchaser who has offered decent money for a horse, 'Well, let's not rush it tonight, he'll look better in the morning.'

Mega-punter and trainer Barney Curley is an ex-monk.

'Why? Because I thought the book of Kells was made by the Sean Graham people!'
(Barney Curley, ex-monk)

Chester has had a racecourse on the same site since 1540, which makes it the oldest in the country.

French jockey Freddie Head has won the Prix de l'Arc de Triomphe for his grandfather Willie, father Alec and sister Criquette.

The father of star French jockey Yves St Martin was a Bordeaux gaoler.

One of TV presenter Brough Scott's most embarrassing moments came while he was on his way to Le Bourget airport. His lunch had included a dicky oyster, and he suddenly realised he was about to be violently sick. With a great effort, he managed to get his head out of the door in the nick of time — just as well, since he was being given a lift by Lord Porchester, the Royal racing manager, in the Royal car.

Lord Oaksey and Brough Scott were once 'accosted' in a 'men only' sauna in Milan.

One of Steve Smith Eccles' hitch-hiking pickups turned out to be a transvestite.

Despite the aristocratic sound of his name, Steve Smith Eccles is a miner's son from Derbyshire.

Captain Becher, to all intents and purposes a professional rider, was given a courtesy title by the Duke of Buckingham which allowed him to ride as a 'gentleman'.

Jem Mason, winner of the first Grand National, once decided to jump a five-bar gate in a race instead of the bullfinch next door, with the explanation that he was going to the opera that night and didn't want to scratch his face. He was sufficiently vain to have the uppers and soles of his boots made by different bootmakers.

John Francome's parents wanted him to become a vet, but with only a low metalwork pass and a lower one in geography this avenue was denied him.
His only previous connection with the horse world was a distant relative who was sent to prison for selling a blind horse as a prospective hunter.

# HORSES

Rheingold's dam Athene was such a hopeless racehorse that she was given away as a two-year-old as first prize in a raffle.

'Foinavon has no chance. Not the boldest of jumpers, he can safely be ignored, even in a race noted for shocks', wrote Charles Benson in the *Daily Express* of 8 April 1967. Because Foinavon was so far behind, he missed the pile-up at the twenty-third fence — the smallest on the course in the Grand National — nipped through, and won at 100-1.

Foinavon was ridden by John Buckingham, who, with his brother, is now a jockey's valet.

Dancing Brave was hit by a car hours before he was due to cover his first mare (at a fee of £120,000), but luckily had no serious damage and the mating took place.

**'Don't worry darling. It was only a minor accident and I made sure the other party was fully covered.'**

# WHAT A FINISH

THEY don't come much closer than this—four nearly in line across the wire in the tightest finish at Aqueduct in New York since 1944.

Girning (second from the top) gets up under jockey Jerry Bailey to lift the first prize by a nostril from K C Turn, on the rails (top).

Another nostril back comes Quietly Bold (No 2), finishing fast on the outside, but just too late and partly obscuring Gnomes Pleasure.

## RESULTS

Lester Piggott never had too many feelings for riders he had 'jocked off'. When he got the ride on Comanche Run that American Darrell McHargue expected, McHargue said he wouldn't even watch the horse in the St Leger, but play tennis. When asked if the rain would affect his ride, Piggott replied, 'No, but it won't half **** up that Yank's game of tennis.'

After a bad run, a jockey explained to his trainer that his horse needed 'firing' (usually an operation to strengthen damaged tendons). The trainer replied that he thought the horse's legs looked fine. 'Between the ears,' the jockey corrected.

In 1988, jockey Ken Morgan dislocated his shoulder (acknowledged as one of the most painful injuries) in the first race of a meeting and rode in the next three races, winning the last. His only comment, 'You don't feel sore when you're warm, but my shoulder really started to hurt after I won the chase and when I began to cool down, I realised I was in trouble.'

The great sporting writer 'Nimrod' opposed chasing as 'that abominably cruel and cocktail practice'. He was also appalled that horses fell in front of viewing ladies.

When steeplechasing became more formalised during the 1860's it was said that the fences at Aintree were too small! It goes without saying that they were a good deal smaller than they are today.

In the early days of racing, trainers were little more than the exercise riders. It was only in 1884 that the trainers of the National winners were regularly recorded. Trainers only began to have to be licensed in 1905.

It was once written by a racing commentator (D.P. Blaine, in the early nineteenth century) that 'the origin of the jockey is in most cases low, and too many of them are not wanting in low cunning'.

Punch

Daughter (at her first race meeting) 'Dressy little man, Donoghue. Turns out in a different costume for each race.'

# ✫ ✫ ✫ ✫ ✫ A JOKE ✫ ✫ ✫ ✫ ✫

There is a popular story of an elderly local steward in the 1920s being questioned by a younger steward, both of whom had seen a horse obviously being 'pulled' by the jockey:

*Young steward:* 'Did you see that?'

*Older steward:* 'Yes, I saw that.'

*Young steward:* 'What are you going to do?'

*Older steward:* 'Back it next time of course.'

✫ ✫ ✫ ✫ ✫ ✫ ✫ ✫ ✫ ✫ ✫ ✫ ✫ ✫

# TRUE FACTS

Prince de Condé built the chateau-like stables in 1730 at Chantilly believing he would be reincarnated as a horse.

Argentinian lads ride work bareback.

Steve Smith Eccles is genuinely interested in bird-watching — the feathered variety.

The night before his ride on Foinavon, the only bed John Buckingham could find was two armchairs pushed together at a friend's house near Liverpool.

At a pre-war race at Hurst Park, an old chaser called Nincompoop fell as for dead at the third last. A vet was called from the ample hospitality facilities and told the groundsman who was comforting the horse that sadly he would need to use the humane killer. With his hand no doubt suffering from port-induced shakes, the vet promptly shot the groundsman through the foot, at which the astonished horse got up and trotted back to the stables.

Horse racing is Britain's fourth biggest industry.

John Francome had his tonsils removed purely to help his breathing while racing.

At one stage, post-war, the trainers' stand at Newmarket was banned to women.

Horse racing was an Olympic sport 600 years BC.

Horses tend to be naturally 'left-handed'.

'chasing.

# THE WAY WE WERE

Sir Ralph Gore was once dining in Newmarket, and, annoyed by the seeming impertinence of a waiter, threw the unfortunate chap through the nearest window. When challenged by the landlord for this behaviour, he simply suggested that the waiter be added to the bill.

The convention of jockeys riding in coloured 'silks' only became widespread in the 1820s. 'Colours' originated from hunting jackets being removed to reveal a coloured waistcoat over different-coloured shirt sleeves.

In the early days, races were run in three heats and owners and friends used to canter behind their horses. The heats could be four-mile races.

In the early nineteenth century horse doping was a capital offence.

Before the war, one young cavalry officer who was a successful amateur had a novel way of converting his 'presents' from grateful owners into cash. When asked what present he wanted, he mentioned a gold cigarette case in a London jeweller's window. The owners would order the case, but since the rider already had one, the jewellers just credited his account.

Steeplechasing (and point-to-pointing) though for long ridden in a form of loose circle, used to be races as described from steeple to steeple and from point to point.

In the nineteenth century horses had open fires in their stables to keep them warm.

Crash caps are now compulsory.

# Factfile FROM THE GUINNESS BOOK OF RECORDS

*VIRAGO*, PROBABLY THE GREATEST FILLY OF THE 19TH CENTURY, WON EPSOM'S CITY AND SURBURBAN HANDICAP AND THE GREAT METROPOLITAN HANDICAP ON THE SAME AFTERNOON A MONTH BEFORE HER 1000 GUINEAS TRIUMPH IN 1854.

THE MOST SUCCESSFUL OWNER OF RACEHORSES THIS CENTURY IN TERMS OF CLASSIC WINNERS WAS THE 17TH EARL OF DERBY (1865 - 1948) WHO, BETWEEN 1910 AND 1945, LED IN 20 CLASSIC WINNERS.

© Guinness Publishing Ltd. 1988

THE 1975 KING GEORGE VI AND QUEEN ELIZABETH STAKES WAS DUBBED BRITAIN'S 'RACE OF THE CENTURY' WHEN *GRUNDY* BEAT *BUSTINO* BY HALF A LENGTH, WHILE THE DISTANT THIRD, *DAHLIA*, ALSO BEAT THE PREVIOUS COURSE RECORD.

Drawn by DICK MILLINGTON

The term 'gingering a horse up' to go faster originated when horses had powdered ginger stuck up their bums to get them going (one way or another).

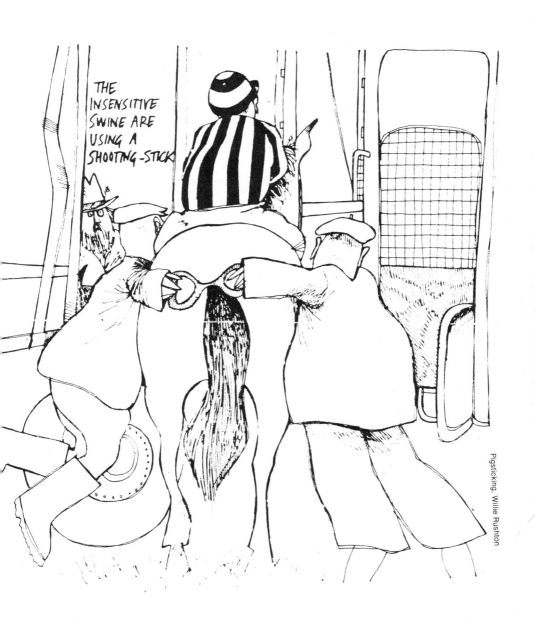

Pigsticking, Willie Rushton

# THINGS THEY SAY

'For every natural jumper there are a dozen with hardly any coordination at all, and the brainless outnumber the intelligent ones by about the same ratio.' John Francome.

When Jenny Pitman returned from holiday and rode out the first morning back, her horse stood on its hind legs and nearly went mad. When she asked when the horse had been out of its stable, the reply was, 'on Saturday morning'. It just happened to be the Saturday morning two weeks before!

Old Harrovian comedian John McCrirrick describing the betting at Sandown for Channel 4: 'And finally, Brough, there are two or three horses in later races being heavily whispered around the ring — what I call "psst" horses.' Brough Scott: 'Well, if we're going to have psst horses the whole thing is going to fall apart.'

John Francome on what it's like to ride a strong horse: 'Keeping him at a sensible pace was like trying to pull a rapist off your mother.'

Trainer Peter Walwyn, known as 'Big Pete', was celebrating a triumph with a French owner, Marc Laloum. M. Laloum, wanting to break the formality of surnames, said 'Je m'appelle Marc', to which Walwyn replied 'Je m'appelle Grand Pete' — a literal translation of which means Big Fart.

Trainers are thought to treat all their owners as mushrooms, 'Keep them in the dark and feed them lots of shit'.

Fishing for compliments, the future Lord Oaksey asked trainer Fulke Walwyn how he did on his first day's riding out, to which he was told, 'You have a good old-fashioned seat — a bit like the one on my lavatory.'

A jockey was about to start in a maiden novices selling chase when he was reprimanded by the local vicar for not going to church. The jockey replied, 'If you'd ever ridden in a maiden novices selling chase you'd realise I can say enough prayers before we jump the first to make up for any amount of missed Sundays!'

'Haven't seen you at church lately, Thomas!'
'I'll be there in a wooden overcoat, vicar if this
one buries me at the first!'

# For
# All Horse Medicines

# You can rely on

# THIS SPORTING LIFE

In 1960 there was a truly poor day's racing at Nottingham. Six races fielded a complete total of 18 runners — with two walk-overs, two fields of three and two of five.

One tested way of pulling off a betting coup was for a horse to be deliberately overladen with lead for a race, never getting placed, therefore not having to weigh in, until the day of the coup, when he would win with correct weights. The winning run would be above board and the connections could clean up.

Riding at Wye one day, jockey Aly Branford fell on a bend, over the running rail. He was twitching ominously when the ambulance services reached him. Apart from breaking a collarbone, he had fallen onto a live electric sheep wire.

One meeting at Zurich has eight races: two trotting, two hurdle, two flat and two chases.

In 1983 Lester Piggott was delayed for over half an hour at the London heliport before riding Teenoso to Derby victory, because a racegoer's top hat had blown into the rotor blades.

The connections of a horse who suspected their jockey had been paid to 'pull' it, greased the reins and the horse duly won.

After enjoying a good session following a jockey's cricket match which turned into an all-night poker school, Terry Biddlecombe was persuaded to pee into a champagne bottle to trick a hungover Macer Gifford — whose only remark on taking a swig was to suggest that it could have been more chilled!

Three jockeys took the inadvisable decision to antagonise the redoubtable Jenny Pitman by stealing the stone cockerel at the entrance to her Weathercock House stables. Mr Plod was summoned, but charges were dropped when Tim Thompson Jones, Simon Sherwood and Jimmy Duggan owned up and each donated £100 to the charity, Riding for the Disabled.

**Steeple chasers are trained to go through their fences.**

Alec Russell

**Jockeys are advised to keep their feet forward.**

"THEY'RE OFF!"

57

# Your titbits...

■ MY wife loves living out her sexual fantasies, and up until now I haven't minded.

Her latest fad is to get me down on all fours while she puts a saddle on my back, jumps on and starts hitting my bottom with a riding crop.

It's all very well for her, but I'm so black and blue I can hardly sit down when I get to the office.

Everybody at work is beginning to get suspicious about me standing over them all the time, but I've really get no alternative. What can I do?

F. R, Lincoln

**FIONA:** *Get the bit between you teeth and give her a ride she'll never forget — the conventional way. That way maybe she'll find horse-riding too dull by comparison.*

Alan Johnson

**Fiona's best advice.**

# THIS SPORTING LIFE

One racing correspondent in 1954 reckoned that Lester Piggott would have to turn to jump racing the following year because of weight.

A handicapper's dream and/or intention is that all the runners in a race should dead-heat.

Perils of the press: In the 1860s, a young English journalist called Dillon was racing correspondent for a Paris paper called *Le Sport*. He was not a great fan of the aristocratic 'gentlemen' riders, and said as much in print. Unfortunately, he was witness to a row between a French Duke, who claimed that a certain English rider, Tom Pickernell, who had beaten him in a race, was really a professional and 'is not entitled to rank as a gentleman in France'. Pickernell couldn't care less, but Dillon unwisely took up his cause in print with an article called 'What is a Gentleman Rider', in which he was rude about the French. The Duke in turn replied with such insults that Dillon's friends persuaded him to challenge the Duke to a duel. Goodbye Dillon!

Another rogue from the old days was Horatio Bottomley. One ruse, having already fixed all the placings in a race, was to then engineer a steward's enquiry, bet on the outcome, and in effect pick up double for the same wager. He came unstuck one day, however, when a horse he had arranged to win dropped dead on the way to the post. The race was a shambles because none of the other jockeys knew what was then supposed to happen.

One jockey was nearly caught illegally gambling at Newbury. He thought he had been spotted by stewards and was indeed called to report to the stewards after the second race. At the time he was wearing a dark suit and trilby. Luckily he lived near the racecourse, so commandeered a taxi, went home, changed, returned to Newbury and reported to the stewards, who accepted their 'mistake' and let him off.

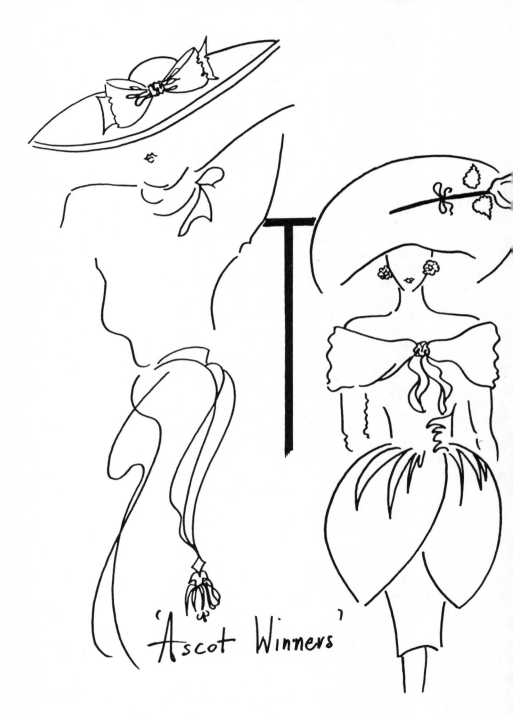

'Ascot Winners'

David Shilling

# THE DERBY

The name of the world's premier flat race was decided by the toss of a coin. The twelfth Earl of Derby and Sir Charles Bunbury thought of the race and first staged it in 1780. Though Bunbury lost the toss, his horse Diomed won the race.

In 1971 Ian Balding had to leave his car in the Derby traffic jam and run to the course to saddle Mill Reef, who won.

There is a superstition about a gypsy boy's grave sited on a crossroads just outside Newmarket. The grave is still tended, and the legend goes that the colours of the flowers on the eve of the Derby will indicate the racing colours of the winner.

The Oaks was first run a year before the inaugural Derby. The race was named after the house rented by the Earl of Derby at Epsom.

In 1984 the Vincent O'Brien-trained Derby odds-on favourite El Gran Señor was beaten in a photo-finish by Secreto, trained by O'Brien junior, David.

The winner of the 1844 Derby — Running Rein — was subsequently discovered to be four years old. Lord George Bentinck, who uncovered the fraud, remarked however that 'If gentlemen condescend to race with blackguards, they must condescend to expect to be cheated.'

Before starting stalls, one Derby in Victorian times had 10 false starts — amid June snow flurries.

# What the trainers say

'He didn't get the trip.'
'Oops, I entered him for the wrong race.'

'He'll be a nice horse, I think a lot of him.'
'I know he's bloody useless, but I bought him.'

'This is the nicest bunch of two-year-olds we've ever had.'

'The owners have paid a fortune for them, so I've got to give them good PR.'

'He/she/it is full of character.'
'I've never met anyone/anything so bloody-minded.'

'He'll run like a Christian.'
'But only God knows how.'

'He ran green. He'll be better for the race.'
'Bullshit baffles brain.'

'He'll be better for the race.'
'There's a fiddle going on.'

'He is expected to give a good account of himself.'
'There's a fiddle going on.'

'He was going well until the last.'
'Races are won by horses and lost by jockeys.'

'If the Jockey Club didn't issue another jockey's licence for five years, there would still be too many jockeys.'

'It'll win a race.'
'No, it won't.'

# PEOPLE

When Fred Archer won the Liverpool Autumn Cup on Stirling in 1873, carrying 9st 4lb, the trainer T. Roughton gave him as a present a short-barrelled polished steel gun — to scare away burglars. It was with this inscribed gun that Archer shot himself at the age of 29.

Fred Archer's battle against the scales drove him to such depression that he shot himself in 1886.

The glamour of a jockey's life was somewhat muted for John Francome when he found himself changing next to one of the top jockeys at his first meeting at Worcester. The top jockey proceeded to inspect himself for crabs.

John Francome broke his wrist on his second ever ride — his first for Fred Winter — falling from King Street in a novice chase at Cheltenham.

After Lester Piggott had nearly lost his ear in a starting stalls accident, he rode a week later in the One Thousand Guineas. At the start, fellow jockey Greville Starkey drew the steward's attention to an ear on the ground — a rubber joke ear dropped by Starkey.

"Allo, 'Allo, 'Allo—what's this 'ear?'

The French jockey Alain Lequeux, whose whip was pinched by Lester Piggott in the closing stages of a Deauville race, got his own back on the subsequently-suspended English jockey by winning the St Leger on Son of Love while Piggott was sidelined. The whip itself was auctioned for charity.

**Riding hands and heels.**

John Francome's first pony had belonged to the milkman's daughter and was called Black Beauty.

# Clichés

'What X doesn't know about horses isn't worth knowing.'

'He weighs six and a half stone wet through.'

'The man himself.'

'However good the jockey, he can't come without the horse.'

'That's how you want 'em — the head of an angel and the backside of a cook.'

'Just what my poor old pa used to say: the head of a lady and the bottom of a cook. Half his horses wouldn't have been good enough to win if they'd started the day before.'

'That horse won as it liked.'

'It couldn't act on the going.'

'But it finished like a train.'

'My grandmother would have won on him today.'

'Your round, I think.'

# APPENDIX.

INTRODUCTION. .. .. .. .. 255

## RECIPES.

---

## OF WORMS.

### (RECIPE, No. 102.)

#### STOMACH DRINK.

TAKE—Tincture of rhubarb, tincture of saffron,
  and sweet spirit of nitre, of each one
  ounce ;
  Gentian root, in powder, one ounce ;
  Peruvian bark, hiera picra, prepared steel,
  in powder, of each half an ounce ;
  Horse-spice, two ounces ;
  Mix the whole in three pints of ale, and di-
  vide into three parts, and give one every
  morning fasting.

Two hours after, give him a mash and warm water. The virtues of that drink deserve the highest commendation in restoring those horses which have been much reduced by some long continued disease : as in lowness of spirits ; debility, and relaxation of the solids ; a loss of appetite ; and for such also as are over ridden, either in the field, or on the road. If the two ounces of horse-spice be omitted, and three cordial balls (No, 90, p. 117) be added, it will make the drink much better.

---

#### BROKEN WIND.

Nitrate of potash, two drachms;
Digitalis powder, one half to one drachm :
Made into a ball with palm oil and linseed
  meal.

We have adopted this treatment for the last fifteen years, with great success and satisfaction. In influenza cases, this treatment is attended with the most happy results. The bleeding and sedative treatment does not answer. No animal can stand so little depletion or weakening of the nervous power as the horse, and such treatment brings on a degree of prostration of nervous power, and irritability of the heart's action, as to prove fatal, or at all events leave a weakened constitution. The diet should be mashes with linseed. Bran ; crushed or scalded oats, occasionally a little malt, aired water, but not to feel warm. If water is made to feel warm, the majority of horses, however thirsty and wishful, will not drink it.

———o———

#### BROKEN WIND.

BROKEN wind, in general, seems to be but little understood by farriers and others. Mr. Gibson says, that hasty feeding a horse for sale causes the

---

#### QUITTORS.

### (RECIPE, No. 162.)

TAKE—Coarse bread, a sufficient quantity ;
  Steep it in old milk for half an hour, then
  boil it to a proper consistence for a poultice ;
  Add common turpentine, and elder oint-
  ment, of each one ounce :
  Mix, and stir them together while warm.

Put the horse's foot into a good sized poultice, made of bran and linseed meal ; pack it well round the coronet, and tie above the pastern.

Either of these poultices may be spread on linen cloth, and applied warm to the part affected, once a day, until the core is ready to be taken out, or falls out of itself : and afterwards dress the wound with the following healing mixture.

### (RECIPE, No. 163.)

TAKE—Egyptiacum, two ounces ;
  Tincture of benzoin, one ounce ;
  Oil of vitriol, one drachm :
  Mix them together by degrees, and put
  them in a bottle for use.

The wound must be dressed once a day with this mixture until it is well.

First, wash the part, and when sufficiently dry rub on the above-mentioned oils (No. 160, p. 209 :)

Saturday's outstanding performance: Jenny Davies on her way to victory in the Haydon ladies' race on Legal Emperor, whose bridle had been shed in a blunder four fences from home. Jenny jumped three fences without steering and took a sharp bend before hitting the front at the last fence.

"You don't get the proper atmosphere in front of the telly!"

Selwyn Photographs

**Walking on water.**

**Walking on air.**

# PEOPLE

Famous flat jockey Steve Donoghue once had a losing run of 112 races.

John Buckingham's career as a valet was helped at the start when another recently-retired jockey, Brough Scott, donated all his racing kit. A valet needs spares of saddles and other bits of paraphernalia to lend to jockeys in his charge.

Michael Scudamore's racing career was nearly ruined by his call-up for National Service. Soldiering only cost him three winners, however, because he was discharged with bad feet twenty-six days later. In that short time, he had put on over a stone.

Josh Gifford once lost a race because his false teeth plate got stuck in his throat after an uncomfortable jump at the last.

On the first day in a new job with Mercy Rimell, amateur and now trainer Nigel Twiston-Davies had such a hangover and felt so ill that he was sick into his crash helmet.

John Francome sportingly stopped riding after he had equalled the injured Peter Scudamore's total in the 1981/82 season, to ensure that they shared the title.

Valets have many tasks. John Buckingham was once asked to glue a trainer's wife's broken fingernail back on.

Ex-jockey and succesful writer Dick Francis still has to tie his arm to his side when he goes to bed to stop his shoulder dislocating — that's his excuse for bondage, anyway!

When Vincent O'Brien was suspended in 1960, he even had to leave his home till the end of the season. His brother Phonsie who stood in then became champion trainer. O'Brien's alleged crime of doping was overturned in court, and he accepted an apology and took no further action.

Raymond Guest, who owned Sir Ivor, was an international polo star and also American Ambassador to Ireland.

Owner Charles Engelhard was Ian Fleming's inspiration for the character Goldfinger.

Joe Mercer survived an air crash at Newbury in 1972.

When 'Jakey' Astor sold his West Ilsley stables to Michael Sobell, it was on the condition that both trainer Dick Hern and jockey Joe Mercer remained.

Steve Cauthen practised his technique riding bales of hay with reins attached to a wall.

# ANOTHER JOKE ☆ ☆ ☆ ☆ ☆

☆ ☆ ☆ ☆ ☆ ☆

Owners are notoriously left in the dark by their trainers. One owner who sometimes used to dine with his trainer to discuss his horses' progress was enquiring about one of his favourites who had recently been injured:

Owner: 'Shall we see him work this morning?'
Trainer: 'No.'
Owner: 'Why isn't he working yet?'
Trainer: 'I shot him three weeks ago. He was useless.'
Owner: 'Why didn't you let me know?'
Trainer: 'I've saved you three weeks' training fees. Do you mean to tell me you would like me to spend another penny ha'penny on a stamp?'

☆ ☆ ☆ ☆ ☆ ☆ ☆ ☆ ☆ ☆ ☆ ☆ ☆

Tony Ederden

**Necking.**

Amateurs used to be referred to as 'gentlemen riders' and until very recently in point-to-points, open races were called 'gentlemen's opens'. However, for some years only one race meeting has had a real gentlemen's race — and that is the Heythrop point-to-point which still run a race exclusively for Old Harrovians and Old Etonians. Good show I say!

**Pecking.**

Impromptu steeplechases were organised by army officers in the Crimea. No doubt any of the participants in the Charge of the Light Brigade who had ridden in the Florence Nightingale Novice Chase would have felt quite at home.

# THINGS THEY SAY

At the first World Jockey's Championship at Cheltenham in April 1984, the then Italian champion Giannantonio Colleo was riding Misty Dale for trainer John Edwards. His bollocking for disobeying riding orders was probably understood as little as the orders themselves, since they were imparted by an interpreter borrowed from a local Spaghetti House.

'Tell him he's a **** and he makes me scream!'

'There are some race meetings to which one takes women, and others, such as Goodwood and Ascot, where women take you.'

'He'll run like a Christian.' This remark by a trainer to Phil Solomons about his horse's chances were rightly countered with 'I don't want him to run like a Christian, I want him to run like a Jew'.

Lambourn stable lad to a well-known Newmarket jockey who wore a hearing aid and had been rude about the lad's favourite filly, 'Shut up and get away from her, you battery-driven bugger.'

'He say your-a-country make-a good ice-cream.'

At one bonfire night party, trainer Nicky Vigors drove a car through the blazing fire. When it was suggested that he might be mad, he replied, 'Not as crazy as you think, it's not my car.'

# PEOPLE

Bruce Hobbs very nearly parted company with Battleship on the way to winning the 1938 Grand National. Fred Rimell, however, upsides on Provocative, leaned over and hauled Bruce back into the saddle. Rimell himself fell two fences further on.

Jockey Geoff Lewis was once a hotel page boy.

Harry Wragg, who rode thirteen classic winners, started his working life in a Sheffield flour mill. On his first morning's work riding, he got kicked on the side of the head and got a fractured skull. He spent five weeks in hospital, but didn't tell his family in case he was asked home.

It took future champion jockey Pat Eddery 50 rides before his first win on Alvaro at Epsom in April 1969, and then five years before his outright championships between 1974 and 1977. He was champion again in 1986.

Racing enthusiasts (they'd need to be) wanting to find Folkestone racecourse should be aware that the course is at a place called Westenhanger — a good seven miles from Folkestone!

Lord Howard de Walden's apricot racing colours were suggested to one of his ancestors by the painter Augustus John as being the best colours for viewing.

Owner Captain Marcos Lemos shares an experience with Mark Twain. Rumours of his death, reported in *The Times* in 1983, were greatly exaggerated.

BBC racing commentators and former jockeys Jimmy Lindley and Richard Pitman sound identical on TV, always dropping the 'g' from words ending in 'ing'.

When John Francome was interviewed by Fred Winter as a possible apprentice, Mr Winter thought that since his hands and feet were so big, he would probably become too heavy to be a jockey.

'Women jockeys! Won't race in my colours unless I find her a matching lipstick.'

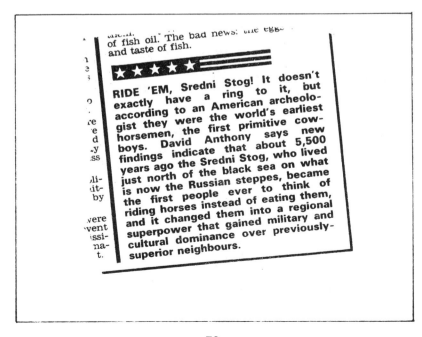

of fish oil. The bad news: the eggs and taste of fish.

**RIDE 'EM, Sredni Stog!** It doesn't exactly have a ring to it, but according to an American archeologist they were the world's earliest horsemen, the first primitive cowboys. David Anthony says new findings indicate that about 5,500 years ago the Sredni Stog, who lived just north of the black sea on what is now the Russian steppes, became the first people ever to think of riding horses instead of eating them, and it changed them into a regional superpower that gained military and cultural dominance over previously-superior neighbours.

# AMBOURN

in Berkshire has been a racing centre for
ons. However, in the 1850's their local vicar, the
obert Milman, was very much anti-racing, and in
p cular anti-gambling. Many of his sermons were about
the evils of the sport. After a big win for the village, some
revellers got into the church and started ringing the bells
at night — they were caught and sent up to the
magistrates.

The racing village of Lambourn was once left by King
Alfred to his wife in his will, along with Wantage, but they
both reverted to the Crown.

In the eighteenth century Lambourn, not Newmarket, was
the national centre of horse racing. The still-existing Red
Lion Hotel was the headquarters for accepting entries, and
racing took place up on the Downs now just used as
training gallops.

Not quite everyone in Lambourn is involved in racing. One
juvenile miscreant claimed he didn't turn up at his
probation office because he was too frightened of the
strings of racehorses passing in front of his house.

In the early days, professional tipsters used to be out on
the Berkshire Downs early in the morning with telescopes
and disguises. Trainers didn't like the intrusion of these
spies, who also leaked information to the press. One trainer
took it so badly he went out on to the Downs and slit his
own throat!

"I guessed that it was
your dad who owned
the stable."

'Can't rely on these damn apprentices now.'

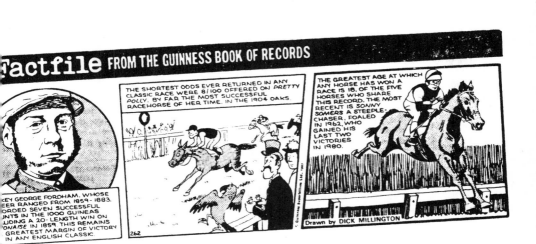

# THE GRAND NATIONAL

Charlotte Brew was the first lady rider to try the National in 1977. Geraldine Rees was the first to complete in 1982.

Dick Saunders was the oldest winning jockey on Grittar in 1982 at the age of 48.

An Irish horse once won the Grand National despite snow on the ground because the trainer had rubbed butter on the horse's hooves to stop the snow balling up.

'Liam did you not take the butter off his feet?'

**Snow shoes.**

# CHIPS WITH EVERYTHING

If a favourite loses a race the jockey is often blamed but in America (where else) robot jockeys now 'ride' miniature race horses, controlled remotely from the stands.

# THINGS THEY SAY

The sister-in-law of a recent Senior Steward of the Jockey Club once described the catering facilities for owners at Newmarket: 'It's just like having lunch in the Servants' Hall.'

After Peter Easterby's filly Mrs McArdy won the 1977 One Thousand Guineas from Luca Cumani's Freeze the Secret, Cumani named his lurcher Easterby, 'then when I'm feeling really annoyed I can kick the dog.'

'A good jockey doesn't need orders and a bad jockey can't carry them out anyway, so it's best not give them any.'
*Lester Piggott.*

Piggott to a trainer whose horse always hung to the left: 'The best thing you can do is put a bit of lead in his right ear to act as a counter-balance . . . with a shot gun.'

Ironic quotation from Charles St George in 1986 about advising Lester Piggott not to take up training, 'They say that I am Lester's financial adviser, but they don't know Lester — he wouldn't take advice from the Governor of the Bank of England.'

Affirmed's trainer said of Steve Cauthen after he had steered the horse to the US Triple Crown in 1978, 'They say Steve is eighteen and comes from the blue grass country, but I don't believe them — he's a hundred and three and comes from another planet.'

Ironic quote by trainer Denys Smith about Lester Piggott's meaness, 'It used to be a game with Lester. I'm sure he tried it on just to see how much he could get away with.'

Peter Christian Barrie, a famous 'ringer', or person who substitutes one horse for a lookalike for a betting coup, was eventually in court for his misdemeanours. When asked by the magistrate what he considered a 'good thing in racing', he replied, 'A useful three-year-old in a moderate two-year-old race, your honour.'

# FIRSTS

The first live radio broadcast of the Grand National was in 1927; the race was won by Sprig.

The first winner of the Hennessy Gold Cup in November 1957 — Mandarin — was owned by the Hennessy family.

Captain Becher had his first ride at Hounslow and also won the first chase to be run at Aintree, though it was not until the first running at that course of the Grand Liverpool Steeplechase that his fall in the brook brought him immortality.

The Grand National was first televised in 1960.

Newmarket's first recorded race was in 1622, and the town still has two separate courses owned by the Jockey Club.

(VIII) Seventeenth Century Prancey or Roly-Pony, invented by Velasquez and useful for caracoling. equestrian statues and other bulbous amenities.

(VII) Fifteenth Century Palfrey or Mediæval Clothes Horse. In the picture the animal is shown pricking-forth In Search of Merry England.

'That'll have to come down Your Grace. The Queen, Princess Anne, Margaret and the Queen Mother— Hot-pants, every man-jack of 'em.'

Tod Sloan of America was mocked at the turn of the century for riding 'like a monkey up a stick', though the stirrups then thought short would be considered quite long today.

Evolution of the American Seat. Getting the weight well forward.

Surtees (of Jorrocks fame) once wrote of steeplechasing, 'that steeplechasing could long stand its ground, even with fair play, was out of the question: at best it was an haemaphrodite sort of business, half hunting, half racing; but the bevy of scamps and vagabonds it brought into the field was enough to drive all respectable competitors out of it and leave the sharks to eat each other'.

Surtees also wrote, 'It is just this mixture of the two sports (hunting and racing) that spoils both . . . it has not the excitement of one, nor the accurate calculating qualities of the other'.

Moving up a tree, getting the weight well up.

In the early days of racing, when thoroughbreds were not a prerequisite, half-bred horses were known as 'cocktails'.

As early as 1810, a marked three-mile course was used for steeplechasing in Bedford, with fences at today's standard height of 4ft 6in. Though eventually there were only two runners, a crowd of 40,000 turned up to watch.

# TRUE FACTS

Within the Rules of Racing, all jockeys who have a fall must report to the Medical Officer. If they happen to have to be carted off the course in an ambulance before reporting, they are theoretically in breach of the rules and liable to a fine.

'I can't wait any longer nurse—when he comes round tell him he's been fined £50!'

# PEOPLE

There were two well-known amateur jockey brothers at the beginning of the century, Frank and Harry Brown. Both tough as old boots. An Irish professional was asked who he thought the best amateur was, 'Well, it depends on how you want them ridden. I would say Harry Brown is certainly the best at stopping them and his brother Frank may be the best when you want them to win.' Harry was in fact more successful, and was only the second rider to become champion jockey, both amateur and outright, in the same year.

Ex-jockey and TV pundit Richard Pitman started wearing a toupee, genuinely believing that no one would notice. He stopped this folly, however, after a day's hunting when, after a tricky jump, both his hat and 'rug' fell off. The 'rug' was promptly 'killed' by a following hound!

Trainer David 'the Duke' Nicholson always wears red socks when he goes racing.

Before 'monkey up a stick' American jockey Tod Sloan rode in races, he worked in a carnival and he loved a bet. When his boss was advertising that he would throw a little boy out of a balloon aided by a parachute designed by the boss, Sloan ventured a wager on the outcome only to discover that he was to be the 'little boy.' He declined the leap.

A nineteenth-century ancestor of Lester Piggott's, John Day II, trained a filly, Virago, to win the City and Surburban and the Great Metropolitan, two Epsom handicaps, in 1854. These two races were only half an hour apart. Virago also went on to win the One Thousand Guineas.

John Francome's first day in a racing stable was nearly his last. He turned on a radio as he was mucking out and several horses in the yard went mad. One galloped all over Mr Winter's lawn.

Enthusiastic, if manic, owner, comedian Freddie Starr can be a nightmare to interview on television, as Central TV's sports reporter Bob Hall discovered.

Freddie decided to call Bob 'Paul' throughout.

**Bob:** How did you first get interested in horse racing?

**FS:** When I was a lad I always wanted to be a jockey, but the rest of my family were boxers — except my dad — he was an Alsatian.

**Bob:** How many horses do you have?

**FS:** I've got four flat horses and all the others are round. All magnificent animals — I like them.

**Bob:** Do the horses like you?

**FS:** I think so. I mean, I've never actually gone up to a horse and whispered 'Do you like me?' You get arrested for that.

**Bob:** What do you get out of horse racing as an owner?

**FS:** Bills.

**Bob:** Do you have a bet?

**FS:** Now and again I have a little flutter — usually it's the heart. It's called punter's shake, not very good when you're holding binoculars.

**Bob:** What about Captiva tonight — does she have a chance?

**FS:** It's her first time out for a year. She's got two bad legs, a dodgy hip and her neck's gone. She's wearing blinkers, a gag and a blindfold. *She must have a chance.*

**Bob:** Thanks, Mr Starr. I'll have a fiver each way.

**FS:** Thanks, Paul, and I do like that dress you're wearing.

The St Leger is the oldest of the English classics, having first been run in 1776 and named after Colonel Anthony St Leger, a local sportsman.

HINTS FOR THE PARK.

# THE GRAND NATIONAL

In 1860 a sporting parson calling himself Ekard (Drake backwards), rode to sixth place in the National on a horse called Bridegroom.

'From frightening obstacles and nasty falls, good Lord deliver us!'

# STREET STEEPLE-CHASES.

THE sport of steeple-chasing having lately become very popular, we beg leave to recommend its adoption in some of our metropolitan thoroughfares. The grand fun of a steeple-chase seems to consist in the risk people run, and the difficulty they encounter in urging their horses across yawning chasms, and other kinds of obstacles. There is often difficulty in selecting a spot where the impediments are sufficiently numerous. We have, therefore, only to suggest the Strand, Holborn, or Oxford Street, one or other of which thoroughfares is always in a condition to admit of the fine old English sport of a steeple-chase.

As the excitement caused by the danger forms the most interesting portion of the pastime, we think the fun of the thing would be greatly enhanced by allowing omnibuses and cabs to take a part in a grand Metropolitan Steeple-chase. The well-known valour of the drivers, who are always ready to outrun discretion, if their horses will gallop fast enough, would induce them to plunge without hesitation into the midst of sewers and gas-pipes, or to go bounding over lumps of granite, blocks of wood, and every other obstacle which the paving, lighting, and watering authorities are so constantly offering to the traffic of the Metropolis.

A steeple-chase from Charing Cross to the Bank, including the delicious bits of wood pavement, here and there, for the horses to slide about upon, and the five or six barriers of one kind or another, that are sure to be in operation in different parts of the projected route, would render it exceedingly well adapted for the purpose we have suggested.

# THE JOCKEY

PADDOCK

MOUNTING

RIDING ROUND
THE PADDOCK

BEFORE
THE START

THE
RACE!

ALL
OVER

RLS

£ £ £ £ £ £ £

One of racing's most expensive disasters was Snaafi Dancer, who cost Sheikh Mohammed $10.2 million at the Keeneland Sales in Kentucky and was so useless it never got on to a racecourse.

A 1985 racing scandal in Hong Kong which parted punters from £850 million was exposed, ending the careers of 11 jockeys, two trainers and a steward. It involved the simple organisation between owners, jockeys and trainers fixing the *places* of a great many races.

An Indian ruler started a stud in 1874 and having seen a horse win at Mooltan Races, offered a considerable sum for the horse to stand as a stallion. The offer was exactly five times what the owner had paid for the horse, so he readily and quickly agreed to the sale. The horse, called Recovery, was a disaster at stud because he'd had a little operation from which he was unlikely to recover — he was a gelding.

£ £ £ £ £ £ £

At Uttoxeter one day, as the riders were approaching the second fence, they saw a man standing in front of it. After much yelling, he got out of the way just in time. On the second circuit, the man was sitting on the guard rail eating his sandwiches. This time he got up and froze to the spot, and the field had to go either side of him.

'Will you look at that—and I've been *starving* meself for this ride!'

Jockeys pay their own travelling expenses — travelling up to 60,000 miles by road a year.

Jockeys' 'civvies' depend on which meetings they are at. At mid-week country meetings they will probably wear open-necked shirts or polo-necked sweaters, but will usually wear suits, or at least jackets and ties, at the bigger meetings.

Forty-eight hours before the 1966 Grand National a carload of jockeys returning from the racecourse to their Southport hotel were involved in a serious crash. One of them, Jeff King, seemed to be dead — but miraculously survived to ride in the big race. Another passenger, Tim Norman, actually won, on Anglo.

Sporting amateur Brod Munro-Wilson's dream of Aintree glory died at the very first fence of the 1980 Grand National when his stirrup iron shattered. Brod jumped the second with one foot in the stirrups and the notoriously-difficult third with no pedals at all — and parted company with Coolishall.

Halt! who goes there?

Odd Bets: In the nineteenth century in Leadville, Colorado, two tarts were matched in a foot race. They raced for the prize of a bottle of Scotch, but most of the population had side bets. The girls raced stark naked, and a man who fell on his knees to pray for the salvation of their souls was quite properly arrested as insane.

A successful nineteenth-century politician in his election address to the voters of North Lincoln wrote:

My horses last year ran 261 times: therefore as the following figures show, they were in the first three 149 times out of 261 starts —

| | |
|---|---|
| Placed first | 64 |
| second | 54 |
| third | 31 |
| Unplaced | 112 |
| TOTAL | 261 |

'Ride 'em out lads!'

The MP was elected with an enormous majority.

# TRUE FACTS

Steeplechasing was only introduced at Ascot in 1965.

It was in 1948 that owners, usually farmers, were allowed 'permits' to train, under Rules, horses owned by themselves and their families. Today's 'permit holders' are often from a similar background.

Crash helmets were only made compulsory in races in 1923 after a Captain Bennett was killed at Aintree. Designs continue to improve. Most jockeys now wear foam-padded vests for extra protection, and these may soon become compulsory. The weight of the helmet (and maybe soon the body protector) are not included in the jockey's weight.

Mechanical starting stalls were only introduced to Britain in 1963.

Betting shops were legalised in 1962.

# LESTER

Sir Gordon Richards didn't reckon Lester Piggott would be able to remain a jockey after 1960, because he thought weight would overcome him.

Lester Piggott won the One Thousand Guineas on Fairy Footsteps, just one week after needing 31 stitches in his ear.

Lester Piggott got into trouble in 1979 at Deauville when battling for second place with a French jockey, Alain Lequeux. He had dropped his own whip earlier in the race, so simply grabbed the Frenchman's to finish second. Not surprisingly, the stewards reversed the order and suspended Piggott for 20 days.

Piggott got Geoff Lewis jocked off two fancied runners at Hamilton Park by ringing the trainer Henry Cecil and saying that Lewis would be riding at Nottingham. Nottingham was a jump meeting!

At one reception in Australia, Lester Piggott was due to speak at a dinner. The person introducing him, however, went on for so long that Lester pretended to slip off to the loo, got into a friend's car and drove back to his hotel and went to bed.

Piggott survived a stewards' enquiry about allegedly hitting a challenging horse's head, with the excuse 'It wasn't a question of me hitting the other horse — its head kept hitting my whip.' The 'wronged' trainer, Bill O'Gorman, came out of the enquiry with the line: 'Christians 0, Lions 7.'

One observer remarked on seeing the eccentric millionairess Dorothy Paget kissing her horse Golden Miller, that it was the first time she had ever kissed a member of the opposite sex — but he was a gelding.

'If you don't let her it'll be the knackers yard for you and the dole queue for me!'

# TRUE FACTS

Newmarket's three main gallop areas in 2,500 acres are claimed to be the largest areas of tended grassland in the world.

**'Faster, Dobson, faster—first lot are due up in five minutes!'**

The grandstand at Longchamps was built farther down the track and then shunted (at the rate of 1.5 metres per hour) into position on rails when ready.

# THE DERBY

The 1913 Derby was full of disasters and oddities. In a fiercely-contested race, the favourite Craganour won by a head, the 100-1 outsider Aboyeur, who had a habit of savaging both riders and horses, which he tried to do in the race when challenged at Tattenham Corner.

Craganour's owner was C. Bower Ismay, who bought the horse as a useless throw-out from Major Eustace Loder's stud. Loder was senior steward on Derby Day and for various reasons wasn't exactly friendly with Ismay.

Aboyeur's owner didn't object to the result, since it was generally accepted that his horse had caused the mêlée. However, for the first time in history, the stewards themselves decided to object to the winner. While all this was going on, it was learned that the suffragette Emily Davidson had thrown herself in front of the King's horse, Anmer, which killer her and brought down the horse and jockey.

Loder almost single-handedly conducted the enquiry and since the main witness was a jockey called Saxby (a Loder protégé) who had been jocked off the favourite, Craganour was placed last, Aboyeur given the race and Loder's decision roundly condemned in the press the next day.

# THE GRAND NATIONAL

In the 1936 Grand National the Honourable Anthony and later Lord, Mildmay, riding 100-1 outsider Davy Jones, was enjoying the trip of a lifetime. For reasons best known to himself, however, he didn't knot the end of his reins — a precaution jockeys always take. At the second last, well in front of the field, the horse made his only mistake. Mildmay correctly let the reins slip through his hands— but the buckle had come undone. Davy Jones ran out at the last. The ordinary chase course at Aintree is now known as the Mildmay Course.

In 1956, the Queen Mother's Devon Loch cleared the last fence in the Grand National well in front, ridden by jockey-turned-thriller-writer Dick Francis. Then inexplicably, with the winning post in sight, the horse spread-eagled on the flat to lose what has since been described as the 'saddest of all Nationals'.

Jenny Pitman was the first woman winning trainer with Corbière in 1983.

Bob Champion won on Aldaniti in 1981, having conquered cancer.

In the 1928 Grand National, a then-record field of 42 runners was led by the front runner Easter Hero. Easter Hero was so far ahead at the Canal Turn, which then had a ditch, that when he straddled the fence it might not have caused too much trouble. However, he slipped back into the ditch and ran up and down, causing understandable mayhem. One rider J.B. Balding, riding his own horse, Drimmod, attempted the fence eight times before calling it a day.

At the second last, the saddle of the strongest-looking survivor of the debacle, Great Span, slipped — unshipping the jockey. This left two horses, Tipperary Tim and Billy Barton, in the race. Billy Barton fell at the last but was remounted to be second of the two finishers.

# PEOPLE

The first day that John Francome rode schooling at Fred Winter's he didn't have a proper crash hat, so he borrowed a motorbike helmet and secured it with baler twine.

A fellow apprentice with John Francome only entered racing because he and his father were compulsive gamblers — he never became a jockey.

After winning the Derby on Troy, Willie Carson put Julian Wilson's top hat over his head 'just to show my head hasn't swollen'. It's not the size of Wilson's head, surely, that keeps his hat up, but his aural appendages.

Jockey Bill Smith's father was a racing cyclist.

Lester Piggott's grandfather, E. Piggott, won the 1912 National on Jerry M. and the 1918 and 1919 Nationals on Poethlyn.

John Francome won a Gold Medal in the Junior European Showjumping Championships in St Moritz, the British Young Riders Championship at Hickstead and also rode in the Hickstead Derby.

What is a 'gentleman' rider? In 1803, a certain Mr Christopher Rowntree was denied first prize in a 'gentleman's' race on the grounds that he was not a gentleman. He took the case to York assizes.
*Case for the organisers:* 'He dined with farmers on market day, paid only two shillings for his meal and wore leather breeches'.
*Case for Mr Rowntree:* 'If he were not a gentleman, he would have paid nothing for his meal and worn no breeches at all.'
'This court finds in favour of Mr Rowntree.'

# POETRY CORNER

The Stewards demand explanations
But listen with cynical looks
It's obvious in their estimation
That trainers are all licensed crooks

Anon.

Many years ago, an amateur rider, Arthur Yates, parted company from his horse on the run-in. However, he grabbed the tail and hauled himself back into the plate to win the race. A ditty was written in his honour:

In racing reports it is oft-time said
A jockey has cleverly won by a head
But Yates has performed, when all other acts fail
A more wonderful feat, for he won by a tail.

Horses are red
Horses are blue
Horses that lose
Are turned into glue

Anon.

# EXCUSES

'He must be a good horse. It took 17 horses to beat him.'
*'Did you ever see such a no-hoper?'*

'He should go better next time out.'
*'The animal can't possibly run slower.'*

'He was always there or thereabouts.'
*'Don't ask me exactly whereabouts.'*

'He didn't get the trip.'
*'The bloody animal wasn't fit enough.'*

'We got boxed in.'
*'I'm an incompetent jockey.'*

'He needed the race.'
*'I'm an incompetent trainer.'*

'We got hemmed in.'
*'We were very unlucky.'*

'The going was too firm.'

'The ground was too soft.'

'He didn't settle.'

'He needs it heavy.'

'A left-handed course didn't suit him.'

'The track was a bit tight.' (Not the jockey?)

Jockey Martin O'Halloran supplements his income by being a horse dentist, usually filling teeth, but sometimes even applying crowns.

**'Ready, steady...'**

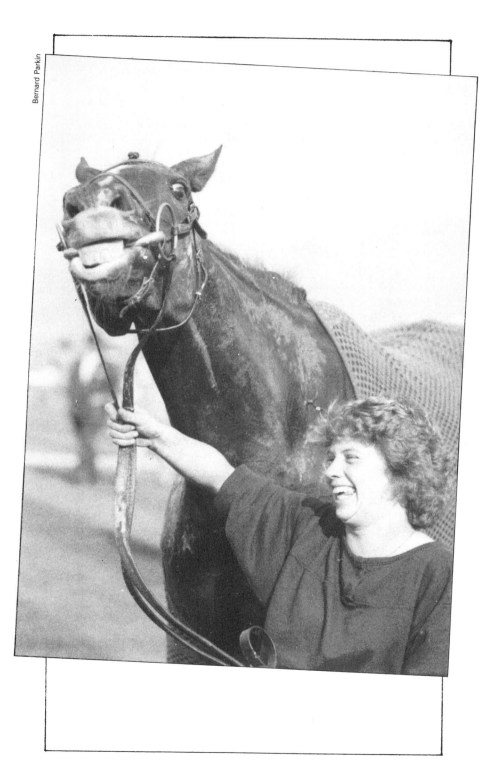

On the Thursday before the 1986 Grand National, jockey Steve Smith Eccles got drunk — then had a row with his girlfriend, who told him to find somewhere to sleep for the night. He drove off to have dinner with local trainer Ginger McCain not far away from Aintree racecourse at Southport. After leaving, he decided to spend the night in the car in his hotel car park, but must have left his keys in the ignition.

Halfway through the night, a teenaged Liverpudlian joyrider decided to take the Mercedes, plus its occupant, for a drive. By the time Steve woke up, he was on the M57, twenty miles from Southport.

The terrified teenager braked and abandoned the car when Steve challenged him — leaving Steve to drive back to the car park!

# TRUE FACTS

Racing in Britain employs directly or indirectly about 250,000 people.

Racing became known as 'the sport of the kings' after the Prince of Wales and the Earl of Arundel had a race in 1337.

Red Rum's trainer Ginger McCain is a Southport second-hand car dealer.

In 1951 the owner of Aintree racecourse, Mrs Mirabel Topham, took the bizarre and ludicrous decision of insisting on doing the radio commentary herself.

A system was briefly introduced in the 1920s which made owners of more than one horse in a race declare which one should win. This was to help punters. Needless to say, however, on several occasions the 'wrong' horse won. Today's Jockey Club Rule 151(i) reads 'every horse which runs in a race shall be run on its merits, whether its owner runs another horse in the race or not'.

*Battle Royal Ascot. Football techniques come to the Sport of Kings.*

# THINGS THEY SAY

A permit trainer from Wales called Bryn Thomas was called in front of the stewards one day at Hereford to explain the disappointing performance of one of his horses. The enquiry was taking time however, and it was getting dark. When he eventually got in front of the stewards, he demanded to know why they were wasting his time.

The stewards explained that even the running of the Queen's horses is sometimes enquired into, to which Bryn replied, 'But when she gets home afterward she hasn't got to milk seventy f***ing cows.'

John Francome referred to one of his main owners, Sheikh Ali Abu Khamsin as 'Sooty' — one way or another, he was sacked as the Sheikh's jockey.

'They all say that Lester is mean, but it isn't true — he's twice as mean as they say.'     *A weighing room jest*

A steward's friendly advice to a jockey who had given a horse a very 'quiet' ride. 'For Christ's sake, if you want to pull a horse, keep your effing elbows going.'

Piggott advises never to catch a loose horse — 'You could end up holding the bloody thing all day.'

Sussex racecourse Plumpton has been described as a bus station with a lawn.

TV commentator Derek Thompson once misread Lord Mildmay's *Times* obituary on Channel 4, stating 'he achieved immorality amongst the English.'

An early racing newspaper called *The Sporting Times* carried the legend 'High Toryism, High Churchism, High Farming and Old Port Forever'.

A jockey who leaves one hand in the air on landing from a jump is deemed to be 'hailing a cab' to regain his balance.

A racing journalist who somewhat erroneously had ambitions as an amateur jockey was put in his place by a fellow scribe in *Tatler*: 'I hear that since Wearing a Crown's owner has taken to riding him in races, the horse's name is to be changed to Carrying a Cross.'

Julian Wilson once referred on television to a virus sweeping through racing yards: 'There's been an effing copedemic'

**An amateur rider.**

# EXCUSES

'We would have won, but the others just went too fast for us.'

'I thought we were going to win four out.' (One jockey imparted this information, having in fact fallen five from home!)

Jockey Brendan Powell once told a West Country trainer whose horse had been tailed off in a novice chase that it could be a good horse 'once it had matured'. The horse was eleven!

Trainer to jockey after a disappointing race, 'Was the going too soft for yours?' 'No, it was the coming back that did us.'

'I don't think he's really in love with the game.'

Bob Champion, who fell at the first fence in the National the year after his fairy-tale win, told his trainer Josh Gifford that it was such a shame, as he had been 'going so well at the time'. (An irony not lost on the author!)

The late Bob Turnell once bollocked a jockey for disobeying instructions by starting a race on the inside rather than the outside. The jockey's excuse was that he thought it had been a right-, not left-, handed course.

◆◆◆◆◆◆◆◆◆◆◆◆◆◆◆◆◆◆◆◆◆◆◆◆

# PERIODICALS

Sam Morshead was riding a horse which would *not* go if hit with a whip. Sam decided to shout at the horse one day, and it duly won. Explaining his tactics to the trainer, he was informed that the horse had had its ears stuffed with cotton wool!

Lambourn trainer Rod Simpson couldn't find any cotton wool for this purpose one day, so sent someone to the Red Cross room to find a couple of tampons, which the horse duly sported with strings flying in the wind.

◆◆◆◆◆◆◆◆◆◆◆◆◆◆◆◆◆◆◆◆◆◆◆

In 1926 Winston Churchill introduced a betting tax — known as the 'bees wax'. Bookies and clients got round this by entering bets at one-hundredth of the value.

Jockey gamesmanship: In a £50,000 Italian steeplechase in 1986, a rival jockey leaned over to grab the challenging horse's bridle to literally hold it back. Not surprisingly, this was noticed and the race awarded to the hampered challenger.

The writer is indebted to scribes Mark Siggers and Chris Williams for an amazing statistic. At the peak of Northern Dancer's career as a stallion, he was worth $20 million per annum per testicle.

When top owners Robert Sangster and Stavros Niarchos realised they were continuing to raise the prices of their purchases by bidding against each other, they not surprisingly decided to join forces.

WHAT ABOUT THESE ALCOHOLICAL STEROIDS, EH?

MADE UP BY THE DIABOLICAL TABLOIDS, SIR

Any racehorse you buy, however cheap, is staggeringly expensive — and fragile in direct ratio.

Many horses bred for racing never see a racecourse and many two-year-olds never race as three-year-olds, having been converted into 'minced morsels' or kebabs.

Those referred to as 'the racing public' consists of those who have never owned, trained or ridden a racehorse.

There are many ways of stopping a horse. He may be pulled up, tied, hooked up, strangled, wangled, hobbled or nobbled.

Surprisingly, a racehorse owning 'syndicate' does not always have Mafia connections.

All racehorse trainers are referred to by their staff and jockeys as the 'Guv'nor' — as a type not (very definitely) to be confused with Her Majesty's representatives on tropical islands.

Jump racing is referred to as 'over the sticks'. Not to be confused with 'Over the Styx', a short mythological ferry-ride to oblivion once you have failed to get 'over the sticks'.

If a horse is referred to as 'green', it usually means it is inexperienced and not from another planet.

A wise trainer's advice to an amateur is to 'put yourself in the best company and your horse in the worst'.

If a horse is said to have 'blown up' it usually means it has run out of breath — not exploded.

# THE WAY WE WERE

It was only in 1970 that the ruling bodies of chasing — The National Hunt Committee — and flat racing — The Jockey Club — amalgamated.

Hunter chases and point-to-points are theoretically restricted to 'bona fide' hunters, but methods of qualifying horses have caused controversy almost since steeplechasing began. In the early days, unscrupulous owners bribed farmers to dig up and kill foxes in front of their horses to satisfy the condition that 'hunters' were required to have been in at the kill of three foxes.

The Grand National Hunt Steeplechase Committee was formed in 1866, but had no formal links with flat racing's already-established Jockey Club. Hurdle racing had been overseen by the Jockey Club, but in 1867 came under jumping rules.

Punch

**Our Overbred Racers**
*(The nightmare of an Anxious Owner)*
'Flash-in-the-pan' suddenly realises the enormous issues depending on him and faints in his trainer's arms.

# WHAT'S IN A NAME

Bad Names: A horse called Passifyoucan was always being overtaken and another called Winagain never won at all.

Willie Carson's middle name is 'Hunter'.

An outside ride for Bill Smith in his first season as jockey for Fulke Walwyn ended in disaster at Fontwell when the horse slipped up on the flat, killed itself, cracked Smith's pelvis and shoulder blade and caused him internal bruising. The horse was called Shattered.

Strange racehorse name: Selrosa (it's an anagram) and KYBO (an acronym for Keep Your Bowels Open).

## CABBAGE PATCH KIDS

John Francome once described stewards as cabbage patch kids.

Even over a hundred years ago, local stewards at race meetings were regarded as incompetents, invited 'to officiate by virtue of their local standing rather than knowledge of the sport or quality of eyesight'.

It has been suggested that the formbook should also be published in Braille for the stewards.

Lester Piggott was suspended 17 times during his career by the English stewards.

Richard Pitman worked for four trainers before riding a winner, after 59 attempts.

Jockey Joe Mercer often used to ride in India during the off-season in England. In 1970 he was convicted of trying to smuggle two diamonds out of Bombay airport and spent three weeks in Poona gaol.

BBC commentator Peter O'Sullevan has on several occasions been able to call in his own horses, notably Be Friendly and Attivo.

It has been said that any jockey sacked by owner Daniel Wildenstein must be good, since he only sacks the best.

A well-known racing crook of the nineteenth century was Robert Ridsdale. He started life as a groom, but by several betting coups had a substantial fortune. His home-bred St Giles won the 1832 Derby, but it was said to have cost him £25,000 in bribes to achieve this — a staggering amount of money in those days. Once people were beginning to rumble him, he found it less easy to work his bribes, and staking his fortune on the 1835 St Leger, lost the lot and had to sell up. One weedy-looking yearling failed to go in his dispersal sale. He kept it, sent it to his brother to train, and it won the 1839 Derby. Nevertheless, many suspected this was a four-year-old ringer. Though Ridsdale won a subsequent court case, it cost him, and when he was found dead some time later in a barn at Newmarket, his wordly possessions totalled a penny halfpenny.

# HORSES

In 1981 the French-trained Vayraan won the Champion Stakes, failed a dope test, but subsequently was allowed to keep the race after a seven-month enquiry which showed he produced his own steroids.

The top German stallion at Graditz, Alchimist, a former German Derby winner, was eaten by advancing Russian troops at the end of the Second World war, thus becoming probably the most expensive steaks ever.

John Henry, the winner of the inaugural Arlington Million, was a gelding — unusual and rather tragic for a flat star.

John Francome's first runner over jumps as a trainer was Crimson Knight, but sadly it fell and died in its box after the race.

IPSWICH RACES, 1849

NACTON CORNER.

W. DOWSING,

OF THE "KING'S ARMS", CORNHILL,

Begs most respectfully to acquaint his Friends and the Public, that he intends fitting up for their accommodation, a

SPACIOUS MARQUEE

At Nacton Corner,

Where they can be supplied with REFRESHMENTS at the most moderate terms.

Wines and Spirits of the very best quality.

EXCELLENT BOTTLED AND DRAUGHT ALES.

PORTER AND STOUT.

PANNIFER, PRINTER, IPSWICH

# Glossary

**BUFFERS**, Jockey Club: damn bad specimens of a damned good breed.

**COLT**: not a Japanese car, but a horse who hasn't been cut off near his prime.

**EXPLANATION**, the stewards recorded the jockey's: they could not prove the misdemeanour they knew he perpetrated

**JOCKEY** (flat): an anorexic dwarf in bright colours who drives a large car with cushions on the seat and blocks on the pedals. In theory, a servant of the owner in a particular race, but almost certainly richer.

**JOCKEY** (jump): punch drunk, nobbly, occasionally toothless, individuals who must be as stupid as they look to take one hundred times as many risks as their flat counterparts for one hundredth (or less) of the rewards.

**OWNER**: someone who can tell you everything s/he knows about horses in under a minute

**PILOT ERROR**: jockey's balls-up

**RAIN**: a typical jumping day in March

**STIPENDIARY STEWARDS**: racing's traffic wardens

**U**: unseated rider (**Non-U**: professional jockey)

**THE END**

JUMP RACING